The Missing Sea

poems by

Kelly Dolejsi

Finishing Line Press
Georgetown, Kentucky

The Missing Sea

This book, my heart, is dedicated to Michael.

Copyright © 2025 by Kelly Dolejsi
ISBN 979-8-89990-290-1 First Edition
All rights reserved under International and Pan-American Copyright Conventions. No part of this book may be reproduced in any manner whatsoever without written permission from the publisher, except in the case of brief quotations embodied in critical articles and reviews.

ACKNOWLEDGMENTS

Many thanks to *Parhelion* for publishing "The Team Player," "The Cartoonist," "The Migraineur," "The Environmentalist," and "The Theologian"; *Green Linden* for publishing "The Guest"; *Metafore* for publishing "The Passenger" and "The Chicken"; and *Red Savina* for publishing "The Realist," "The Arborist," "The Patient," "The Beautician," and "The Climber."

Publisher: Leah Huete de Maines
Editor: Christen Kincaid
Cover Art: Family snapshot by Susan LeVan
Interior Art: Jen Jordan
Author Photo: Kelly Dolejsi
Cover Design: Elizabeth Maines McCleavy

Order online: www.finishinglinepress.com
          also available on amazon.com

                Author inquiries and mail orders:
                      Finishing Line Press
                        PO Box 1626
                Georgetown, Kentucky 40324
                            USA

Contents

Part 1: The Captain
The Captain 1
The Shark 2
The Landlord 3
The Seismologist 4
The Hippie 5
The Team Player 6
The Editor 8
The Cartoonist 10
The Mnemonist 12

Part 2: The Chicken
The Chicken 15
The Exterminator 16
The Migraineur 17
The Courier 18
The Woodsman 19
The Environmentalist 20
The Passenger 21
The Arborist 22
The Guest 23
The Sailor 24

Part 3: The Mammal
The Mammal 29
The Driver 30
The Arsonist 31
The Existentialist 32
The Performer 33
The Neurosurgeon 34
The Theologian 35
The Footnote 36
The Conductor 37
The Realist 38

Part 4: The Constable
The Constable 41
The Concierge 42

The Nurse 43
The Renter 44
The Composer 45
The Climber 46
The Salesperson 47
The Gardener 48
The Actor 49
The Teller 50
The Prostitute 51

Part 5: The Pharmacologist
The Pharmacologist 55
The Dog-Sitter 56
The Reader 57
The Ornithologist 58
The Barber 59
The Hydrologist 60
The Plumber 61
The Mourner 62
The Beautician 64
The Cheesemonger 65

Part 6: The Mother
The Mother 69
The Gadabout 70
The Civil Engineer 71
The Prize 72
The Meteorologist 73
The Dreamer 74
The Doctor 75
The Astronomer 76
The Zookeeper 77
The Robin 79

Part 1: The Captain

The Captain

She's the only child on a boat bloated
with grown-ups. A dumb boat: no water

anywhere, no view at all—she's surrounded
by nothing, blank white walls blocking

a horizon, a sun, maybe whales. She wakes
to a blizzard that has filled the windows

of their ground-floor apartment with snow,
thick and lightless. The dream continues,

or the feeling from it, as she eats oatmeal
in her ruffly blue nightgown. She knows

there's a whole world somewhere—a bike,
a street, a bunch of kids—that's been lost.

Where did it go? Will it come back? Will she
ever again be open and vast and free?

The Shark

She learns to make her mom's drink:
two parts whiskey, one part sweet

vermouth, measuring with the red lines
on the liquid measuring cup, the same

she uses for pancakes. Her dad's drink
is just: bring the can from the fridge.

She carries both downstairs to the bar
in their new house. On football days,

she also gets to spin on a stool, play penny
poker, coins clattering along shiny wood

or better, stacked in immaculate piles.
She gets to watch the game with Dad,

which means he laughs when she yells
what he yells. Which means all is well.

The Landlord

The girl folds the red paper in half,
carefully cuts the curve at the top, trying

to make it pretty, like the slide of a rainbow,
the seat of a cloud. *This is the left ventricle,*

she whispers, the words pumping like blood
inside her. Mrs. B said the left ventricle is big

and strong. To her it is alive, an animal, a lost-
and-found dog like the huge brown labrador

sleeping in her kitchen at home, the dirty dog
her dad found abandoned in the hardware store

parking lot last night, the big-eyed stinky mess
she already loves, has already named. *This is*

Sandy. The scissors succeed. The red edge rips
slowly, and the cut part does not bleed.

The Seismologist

She had a bad day at school. Now squats
like children do in the doorway, a future

geologist, thinking how she might enjoy
an earthquake. She wants to be comforted.

She doesn't know how to ask. Looking up
at her parents, where they perch on stools

with cigarettes and golden drinks, she wonders,
In a catastrophe, could I save them? Mom says,

"Go do your homework." They laugh, and
the girl walks away while Dad holds up his

finger and thumb as though they play a violin,
asks, "Want some cheese with that whine?"

If the quake strikes now, to get to her parents
she'll have the stairs to contend with, too.

The Hippie

The three of them love Carole, voice
like warm cider by a fireplace, like something

perfect squared, lyrics so poetic she feels
in her 13-year-old heart, *I am a natural woman.*

Tonight, her dad plays the record again.
Her parents drink quietly. She's on the floor

in a luxury of dogs. As the third track begins,
her dad closes his eyes, his lips forming

Carole's words around the pumpkiny filter
of his cigarette. The refrain comes around,

Carole sings, "It's too late," and her mom
is sobbing. Her mom says, "How could you

fucking do this to me?" her eyes blue-flaming
in the sudden aching silence of their home.

The Team Player

"Mustn't" is a mantra, the continuation
of her long adolescence, endless semesters

afraid of her armpits, nipples, white pants,
and the way her thighs pucker across a chair.

Her friend has hair on her chin and the boys
say she "cultivates it." *Why can't I be transparent?*

she thinks, though when they ignore her
she wishes to be stared at like an accident.

She mustn't be artlessly hostile, mustn't tell
on her parents—for what exactly?—or on

herself for allowing it. She feels awe when a girl
on her track team calls going to school or

home suicide. She opens her mouth and fog
comes out, not on cat feet but elephant.

The Editor

The blurry too-closeness of her, flown off
a swing we are too old for, hot, thirsty, soft,

salty. The whoosh of *This is why bees buzz.*
I feel her Chuck Taylors wedged tightly

between my own, her fingers pouring down
my bare summer back as we spin beneath

monkey bars and lightyears of empty space.
I already know I'll remember this at 90,

blowing out my candles. The kiss ends like
dreams, before the apogee, and soon I head

to the desert—sharp plants, sharp months
of reaching out with a blue pen and lined paper,

my heart swelling, contracting, directing its river
in loops that carve the rest of me away.

The Cartoonist

Panel one shows a small girl with a man
cutting down a tree. On the drive home

they stop in a parking lot, tree in the bed
of the truck. Cut to him in his sweatpants

passing through the automatic door, the girl
following inside to return beer cans. At home,

a tree stuffed with angels, closeups of his
beard, pine needles, his brown eyes staring

out the frame, a cigarette, a hand shaking with
its mini glass. The girl in bed. She wakes. Cut

to the halo of elastic around his ankles as he sleeps
beside the toilet. His vaporous arms around her

as they dance at her wedding, his fine suit,
his *I don't need to worry about you anymore.*

The Mnemonist

One morning time snaps like stale bread
and everything falls out of order, drops

in a huge tangle. Childhood bucks forward
to deathbed and right-now thins to air

between the crumbs. Something ceases.
It ends inside of her body, the way a trail

full-stops at an overlook, a cliff, one step
to more end. She may have stared inside

her eyelids, or at the ceiling. She doesn't
remember. She drives home after but also

doesn't. She also curls like a baby plant
in a dry seed. She doesn't tell her mom

or write in her journal. She carries on
from inside the most ruby-throated bird.

Part 2: The Chicken

The Chicken

It isn't only the red cart, I think:
The white chickens are also wet. And so

the chickens begin to shower with me.
To stare at me eating my eggs. When it

actually rains, we all putter around
in the warm kitchen, searching for vanilla,

folding in blueberries. Clucking as muffins
rise like brown water in the arroyo, their

blueberries exuberant as tumbling plastic.
People like best what they easily remember,

I think, and sit with the bantams
to write a long, difficult poem, sometimes

gazing out at a gray afternoon, at downfall
disguised as weather, or as an image.

The Exterminator

Something uninvited burrows into my skin
at the base of my skull so smoothly I feel

nothing until I find the mass of not-me,
red and itchy, unremitting, not a tumor,

thank god, but a nag. I become familiar
with the tender spot, used to it, pained

but also proud to have a secret, this *other*
that is also me, a remote and alien world

but also my body. Still, you know, I cry.
I try sports, popularity, ecstasy in pill form.

I try marriage and children. It stays. I take
to wearing hats. Smiling no matter how it

or I am feeling. Praying a larva will emerge
onto my pillow, and I won't be able to save it.

The Migraineur

I get up for warm oatmeal or tea,
but my legs are eyes, my belly a troubled

urn of endlessly winking eyelids. I tilt
toward the sink, a rack of cups, the seizing

spider plant and disco-beaming sponge.
The window hovers, its glass grazes on

lemony purslane that used to be grass.
The sun putters. I lean like a waiting

thing, an umbrella, a racquet, and see
the smallest physics of light: each particle

in private agitation, its own discrete eternity.
A twitching blue flame, a trembling

turquoise kettle, each warm atom within
powerless to slow down or to disappear.

The Courier

I bike miles past the last structure into
nowhere, the sky as kind and private

as the underside of a blue hydrangea,
daylight filtered through vaporous petals.

What do I need? Call it a bigger pot.
A warm and well-pined syllabus. In my ears,

a voice shivers like a shiny indigo brush
in a child's hand, its singer visible in my mind:

blonde, gorgeous in his sweater and smoke.
Call it a vanity of clouds, concession of pedals

to body, body to vanishing point. Morning
blooms, swoons, dark elk wandering like gods.

I forget everything but the ground rising,
falling. Breathe with the road and land.

The Woodsman

The strawberry moon, the berries-ripen
moon melts slow and fat across the cloudless

griddle, a long dark nowhere above black
triangles of dense trees like symbols of trees,

which stand in a row beyond hard, nearly
vertebrate tussocks of grass in the meadow.

I hold my husband's hand and move slowly
along the rocky trail. The kids' headlamps

wobble like lightning bugs far in front
as we drift into the plush geometry

of ponderosas, breeze-twittered aspens.
I think of my dad, who believed in visitors

from other planets. Of Young Goodman Brown,
who got lost. I see how it could happen.

The Environmentalist

More than 40,000 penguins rescued from
a single oil spill. The Asian Unicorn, first

discovered on a hunter's wall. My mother's
moonlit stories. Donald Duck and the alleged

malapropism. Abduction and the mountain cow.
My mother needs surgery. She doesn't want

to tell me the risks. The solemn northern
sportive lemur, homesick. The world's two

remaining Northern White Rhinos, both
female. *I may lose my voice*, Mom texts,

syllables fording the multiverse between
my mother's hand and my own. Pangolins

poached for their armor. Christopher Cross
in the tape deck from Arizona to New York.

The Passenger

Instead of my body, I find instructions
for a bird feeder. Glitter paint, a milk quart,

sunflower seeds, a finch, and one hour
with 4-year-old Jocelyne. Instead of a soul,

a verbose description of a strawberry moon,
a stock photo of its inverse pupil low over

a Swedish lake. Instead of my voice,
a missing boy, age 11, black baseball cap,

and I tell him going home may refer to
1 Film; 2 Literature; 3 Music; 3.1 The long

yet undeterred migration of the Arctic Tern.
Instead of my heart, 23 [REALLY] fun things

to do when you're on the edge of a lonely abyss.
Instead of enlightenment, Kayak.com. The sky.

The Arborist

From the snug rented parabolas
of a driver's seat, from the driveway,

x number of feet from the front stoop,
which she is also meeting—hello

concrete stairs and glass dragonfly!—
she sees her mother's cheeks, formerly

some function of pi plus memory, now
closer to what detaches in pink threads

off a spring tree, floats and disappears
in the green heat. A hint of the body

y inches below, a continuum of wild fluff,
too light to remain on surfaces for long.

She is smoke before the cigarette.
There is no one left to forgive.

The Guest

Who am I? she asks in the guest room
at her mother's house. Who's asking?

she thinks. There is nothing she
mustn't do. As of yesterday, beginning

officially in a room lined with posters
of nostrils, her mother has cancer,

the rooms of her throat full of cells
building more rooms filled with stacks

of cells, cancer like a child playing with
blocks of her loved one on the floor,

while the doctors spoke over its head.
What's my purpose? she asks. For what

am I thankful? Her mother: full of coffee,
smoke, and strangers, like the Enlightenment.

The Sailor

In the dark, the boat is a kind of a whale,
the broken kind, a wooden mammal

vanquished against some shore. No more
warm blood, live births, swimming.

The boat's bones lean into blank, dead
space. Onboard, adults flood the deck

like bristle worms, laughing, drinking.
I'm the only child. I wish *no please not*

this time but still a red dot appears on the back
of my smooth hand. The deck is wide,

inescapable. There is no edge to the boat,
the whale, my small body. There is no sea

for dreams. I infect every adult before I wake,
my head beached, sure they'll hunt me down.

Part 3: The Mammal

The Mammal

Bad news cycle. She drives to the hospital
thinking every man is the worst. She parks

near the pink posts, thinking every man
she ever met has raped or not said anything

to stop his buddy. Inside, she worries even
about the sweet old ones. The female technician,

Doris, presses her breast repeatedly, hard.
Women expect rape. They wear whistles.

unflattering clothes. But she's heard police
describe victims' sweatpants as "easy access."

After the ultrasound, she carries her shirt, purse
to the adjoining room and wipes the hot gel

from her boob. A man peeks in, asks, "Are you
all alone here?" He'll be doing her biopsy.

The Driver

Her mother has thinned into a cirrus,
a collection of evaporating ribs and

cigarettes that releases thunderous coughs
into a paper towel. The daughter forgets

to worry about smoke in the rental.
She pushes the gas pedal, observes

road signs, follows her mother's quiet,
almost secret directions, praises the happy

convenience of the cancer center. She enters
past a long row of blue folded wheelchairs

without folding, laughs when her mother
has a hug but no gift for the radiologist's

birthday. She watches a hard white mask
erase her mother's face.

The Arsonist

Outside the airport, my mother writes
Peoria Peoria Ouch. Or something like

that. Her handwriting is terrible. I don't
ask. I open my arms. I remember

a pigeon I nursed to health as a child,
so thin inside its feathers.

I hug her again, cradling her bones
against my wealth of fat. Somehow

I walk away. In my seat, I still feel
her shoulder blades in my empty hands.

I have loved her wings right off.
Again I think of the pigeon, Beatrice,

the funeral we held behind the shed, singing
Mine eyes have seen the glory of the burning of the school.

The Existentialist

Another dog sent home, this time to a land
of bone broth. Iris, with your one-eighth

of one blue eye, with your wild bladder
and dry mouth, your sleeping cage and

your fur like velour, like fuzzy new grass.
The dogs go home. Many happy returns.

She dreams the obvious: her own. Perpetuity.
The snow comes down, pieces of other,

shavings from some godlike frozen pencil,
and what else would it write on Pueblo Dr?

More, *more, more*. Iris, chewer of book corners
and floor boards, licker of cupboard doors,

good-bye. *Baby, it's a brand new day*, she sings
over the vacuum, over the beat in her chest.

The Performer

Her biopsy occurs beside a framed print
of a painting of a field. Not a real painting,

no linseed, nor palette, nor for that matter
petals. The removal of removal would place

her in the 19th century amid sloping wild poppies
beside her mother, who lowers her parasol

as clouds float like parasols, Magritte-style.
If all removal were removed she would be in

Monet's brain or hands or lungs. Her breast
would not be breast tissue, would instead

be a round drop of turpentine on the grass.
Benign. Penumbra. Palimpsest. Parsimonious

step toward abstraction while a machine grips
her breast in mid-clap, unable quite to cheer.

The Neurosurgeon

For almost five years after her father
climbed into the clouds and changed

into his white costume, she didn't
believe her mom would die, too. This

eventual necrosis she packed into one
rather unattended neuron, in vaguely

the same area as *Beowulf*, important but
impersonal. Even after the diagnosis,

she doesn't get it. She parks the rental
and once more sees her mother's face

through the screen door. Cheeks lost
at sea. Body like the third side of a coin.

Never questions whether the voice
called "I" belongs to her or to *her*.

The Theologian

This morning, I become a co-signer
on the bank accounts. Agree to give

Mom's boyfriend the car, but to sell
the trailer. Find out my mom believes

my dad returns as a hawk, as many hawks.
A cast, a boil, a kettle, a screw of hawks.

I massage my mother's back, seeking
each fading patch of muscle, listening

for her relief. I used to hate the sound
of her pleasure, I remember, surrounded

by pills, tubing, ashtrays, Dan's ex-wife's
ceramic owls, and yes the punchbowl

I've always known I'd inherit. Even so,
there will come a time you can't believe it's you.

The Footnote

Cold weather, and the at-once familiar
sound of the heater, enthusiastic to be

breathing again. After the first biopsy,
the tech had put an asterisk of blood-stained

tape on her breast—a literary reference,
Michael says, *Breakfast of Champions.*

It's there for a week, in the shower,
during sex, while she rides her bike,

while she reads mom's text about the trach
as well as updates on Tara's mom, who

passed quickly. Meanwhile, autumn keeps
crafting away in the front yard, first

in delicate branches, soon everywhere,
yellow silk in the most complicated patterns.

The Conductor

It could be my own heart gone
feral, the blitz of my own lame

agony, maybe the other shoe
blatantly resounding through

the pines, a migraine *al fresco*.
But it's not fading, it's not eased

by triptans, it's as outside as a
thunder storm, proud and forcing

me to pay attention, making me
decide: what is inside my head

and what is truly a mob of students
blasting Sousa and oh god no

it's Sweet Caroline. Kids, practicing
for the game or just expressing joy.

The Realist

I read that by the time Magritte was 21,
five of his siblings and his mother were dead.

No, it wasn't Magritte. But by the time
Magritte was 13, his mother had drowned

herself in a Belgian waffle. Obviously not.
By the time I remember it was Kierkegaard,

it wasn't Kierkegaard. Magritte also worked
for a wallpaper factory. But not yet. He also

was present when his mother washed up near
their home. He also wasn't present. Her white

dress wasn't covering her face like an apple
or dove or cloth. He didn't die immediately

from pancreatic cancer. He didn't steal clouds
from the river. He wasn't even Magritte.

Part 4: The Constable

The Constable

While my daughter finally resigns
herself to a banana, my mother sends

66 words. My thumbs go dream-slow,
tap out, *So no surgery?* I know what

this means. My other kid comes in,
crouches near the pantry, unwilling

to put away her dinner dishes from
last night. A voice in my mind yells,

"Hark, the police!" I know what
this means. I'm the only one trying

to keep my mom alive. I'm 8 again,
worried my parents won't escape

if there's a fire. I'm also here, with
my kids, on a sunny summer day.

The Concierge

Somehow her mother goes from
dying in the graceful abstract

to dying in a 12 x 12 room,
a machine inflating her lungs

alongside a dozen IV and other tubes
that start to look like pasta slowly

tumbling off some unseen plate.
Nurses play with the noodles.

Doctors give her their cards.
The word *hospice* is a room. *Time*

a fleabag motel. *Daughter* a painfully
organized closet. Soon she gets a room

in the good hospital, where they
cut a good hole in her neck.

The Nurse

She re-enters the hallway. My *mom
is really having trouble breathing*, she says,

to the same nurse as last time. Marc.
He glances at her mother gasping away

on the white bed. She lays her head
by her mother's blanketed legs as voices

stay well above her and comfortably
dressed feet wheel in more tables.

The cool quiet sheet. The silk of her
mother's hand. Two nights in the ICU

before the miracle of taking her mother
home, her mother as light and heavenly

as an origami crane, a paper crane
who demands an ocean of vodka.

The Renter

My mother finds an apartment,
everything empty, peering back at her,

a 600-square-foot eye with deep soul-like
closets, with room for her shoes and

a mop. *Hospice nurse comes Tuesday.* I never
thought I'd miss her trailer but at least there

she didn't need permission to light candles.
We stand in the parking lot so she can smoke

while the neighbor glares from the hole
in my mother's throat to the tip of her Camel

and back again. We ignore her, keep making
our plans. I drive Mom to the antique shop

on E. Main, where we buy the lamps
she loves instead of ones she can afford.

The Composer

Now, the Bach prelude almost
makes me cry. I am so disgustingly

alive. My heart sprouts bicycle tires,
my breath behind it like a shameless

golden dog. I want so badly to share
the feeling. To share something.

Perhaps my mother will read Woolf
now that she's on morphine. Perhaps

she'll begin quoting Sandburg as soon as
she wakes up. We sit across from each

other in the new apartment, one slumped
and snoring quietly, one holding a book,

while a study in C major folds over us
and the world opens for a moment.

The Climber

In what's called a *flow state* one must
sharpen, one must move, there is nothing

but the work. In a world of bullshit.
New bomb scare victims. What I want

is to live in the span between what
happens. To fill space without time.

To lengthen without longing. Only
the word *and*. The *n*, the +, the &.

The eye of rhetoric, mobs, terror,
news. Love without calendars. Nothing

sacred about finishing a sentence,
hurrying to the end of a hug, surveying

the canyon up high like a falcon
that never lets go of its prey.

The Salesperson

Angry. Lonely. Appalled by my own
vagueness. Poems don't. Words don't.

Language was never the answer. "Peacherino"
will someday make me swoon but today

place order. It's a philosophical impossibility
but nevertheless, the shirts will come.

My gaze wanders to the cluster of birds
outside the glass, their feathers flashing

like quarters in the low morning sun, and
god, those glamorous, wound-tinted throats.

The shirts will move from shelf to human hands
to flying box to right here, my table, sunlight

flickering in. I'll cut the tape and then who
will I be, pulling such colors tenderly over me?

The Gardener

After extensive searching, her left
breast does not. Her mother's throat,

though. Christie's salivary gland. Kate's
and Katy's husbands, Bill and David.

Another friend's mother, another breast,
another liver. Lynette's back. And now

Larry. The church empties. The doctor
treats the patient; poem and song treat

the bereaved. One sister and one flute.
When the geranium leaves turn amber

and glow translucent in the late winter
sun, what happens to the gardener?

Her breast with its amber, a fine little dot,
her mother's voice burrowing into the pot.

The Actor

Hell Sunday is Sunday. But this
is Saturday, and a real funeral not

theater. *Theater has all the basic elements
of a family.* She usually bought tickets

to see him, collected his quotes for
the features page: *One doesn't really

have to think for this play.* When they
rehearsed together for her acting

debut, she was scared. He said,
theater is a team sport. He told her to

*go ahead and be a bitch. The audience
will enjoy being offended.* She doesn't

recognize the Larry described here.
Slapstick without the slap.

The Teller

This time, the dreaming happens
on the rock wall with a bolt and

ratchet. A cool Monday blowing
wet snow down a paved sky outside

the big windows. Climbing accident,
she calls it, though it is a misfortune

of longing, and now the red dot of her
childhood nightmare—the mark,

the contagion, the blame—has migrated
to her face. This time, she enjoys

going to the bank with the blood still
sticky and gleaming, enjoys the teller's

fear. "Look," she says to the woman
with the drawn-on eyebrows. "I'm real."

The Prostitute

Enjoy the innocence, she says. Her mother
is dead. Mine has a few more months.

The fuzzy catkins hang like rabbit's feet
on every branch of my aspen tree, and

are opening into hundreds of tiny leaves,
the new palette impossibly hopeful,

like Holden Caulfield's prostitute's dress,
as if the tree fills day by day with dresses,

each soft and silent, waiting for a girl to
cover up. A man in a white pickup sees me

standing alone in the sunshine, gripping
a cluster of green between my fingers;

I wave as guilty people do. She says,
You don't know how awful it can get.

Part 5: The Pharmacologist

Part 3: The Pharmacologist

The Pharmacologist

Sleep like a cut fruit, the core removed,
and she stumbles to the bathroom,

blind in the rubbery hovering lights
but already relieved, certain what

she needs, convinced the migraine
is to blame for everything—not only

the bruised goo of 4 a.m. but every
bad poem, every slow brain cell that

tomorrow will choose YouTube over
Gertrude Stein during the one hour

she has to read. The sappy beetle-bored
pine trunk of her mouth bends toward

the primeval faucet, its stream even and
dreamy as a sprinkler system in a forest.

The Dog-Sitter

After a week of silence, her mother writes,
a little sad. The mountains wear cumulus

pajamas, and it's time for bed all day long.
A dog the size of a spinet piano lies at her feet,

pining for an energetic couple visiting
their grandkids. A borrowed dog, blue-silver,

tarnished-silver, waiting for her to give up
the couch. He really is immense, a great dane,

so similar to one that used to be hers.
She strokes the warm fur, enjoying

the evocation of a dog at hand. *A little sad.*
She sends her mother a photo of a dog that

isn't her dog, and gives him the couch,
and gives him her arms, and gives him her face.

The Reader

Her death won't be a big deal, no
worse than childhood, which, well,

maybe wasn't that bad. Right? I say
this again to Michael while the suet

draws jays as though taking a blue
pencil to the air—a blue that could

only happen on a Saturday in autumn
after an overnight rain. I'd grieved

my mother by knowing her, I tell him,
his big, sweet arms holding me. What

can I miss later that I don't miss now?
I want to complain, but instead I watch

the jays, and think how it feels to be wrong
about everything and still be loved like this.

The Ornithologist

Rude Parrot. Hell Chicken. Off Color
Jerk Bird. All lined up in gleaming coops

with removable heads. Founts flavored
like caramelized bananas, molasses,

pound cake, pears, licorice, blue agave,
peaches. Grey Geese distilled, stilled,

shelved, sold. Famous Grouse flushed
and silken beneath long, fluorescent suns.

Is that my father in his billowing gray
sweatpants, gray flannel shirt, red beard,

whispering to a six-pack of Crafty Old
Hen? Kentucky Owl, Old Crow, tell me

more. I keep losing him in bubbles.
Why now? Why must I lose him again?

The Barber

I would never miss her. My only
regret is that I can't keep cutting.

That I can't live in the bathroom
with the buzzing and the music

and no one else to worry about.
Hair falls to my shoulders, the floor,

the trash bin, landing silently,
as happy to be in a plastic bag

as on my head. I keep singing.
My voice has never sounded so

much like a sound I want to hear.
Press the clippers against my

head and watch the woman
in the mirror go away.

The Hydrologist

First school starts. Then it is snowing.
My daughters outgrow all their sleeves,

surpass me on the piano. My mother
sends one word: *Tired*. An ambulance

eats Thanksgiving. A land-locked octopus
of sterile tubing and nurse arms steals

my mom's humanity but at least she's
breathing. They release her, I go home,

and it's still snowing. Our driveway
deepens, the foster pug tunnels through

like an endoscope, the car can't make it up
the hill, no one leaves for a week,

the snow no more than an annex of my
mind, but it's annexes all the way down.

The Plumber

Part of her kissed her daughters
and husband. Part of her stayed

in Palmyra, NY, on the narrow
white bed near her mother's wicker

thighs, watching the changing
numbers. Part of her went home,

shopped, wrapped, dreaded festivity,
the lights, her late father's birthday.

Part listened for the inevitable call
from a canyon wren singing an endless

decrescendo. Part wanted a drink:
her mother's drink, only she would

pour it down the sink, make another,
breathe it in, pour it down the sink.

The Mourner

She sits quietly in the pew, listening
to Pachelbel on viola, browsing the slim

order of service for the father of a friend
who loved his work, his children, and,

it states, reading and watching birds—
at once she sees them: a library of fat doves,

of house finches and chipping sparrows,
dusky hazel plumes gorged with paragraphs,

epithets, unreliable narration one can discern
with high-power binoculars, rose-throated

light verse sleeping on wires, cinnamon-
feathered sonnets bobbing in the pines,

the crisp flapping wings of the climax
rising silently outside the church window.

The Beautician

She feels an almost an erotic desire to
give in to aging, to stay still when she

can move, to stiffen when she can
stretch, to cut her hair when she can

write. *My mother is dying*, she tries to
admit. No, not dying. A survivor, done

with chemo now, her golden leaves
not decaying, not softening beneath

an early snow. Her golden leaves glow
on the silver living tree. She waters red

geraniums in the greenhouse or she
forgets and they flower on. Life conspires

against itself, but she lives, hundreds
of branches nodding *yes yes* in the wind.

The Cheesemonger

During the final conversation with
the doctor, I think of Raskolnikov

walking up the stairs, a bag of bread
and cheese cradled against his chest,

babelike. I think of the the paper bag
crinkling, the stairway bleak and murder

waiting—Dostoevsky's plot waiting.
Hard yellow cheese, pungent, obscuring

the scents of the poor Russians who live
in the building. Thick rigid bread, mostly

crust. The heaviness of the man's steps
as he climbs toward what has to happen.

I hear the words, *A decision must be made.*
Raskolnikov must arrive at the door.

Part 6: The Mother

The Mother

When mothers die all sorts of days
are in progress. The white dog

curling in the deep indentation
of a green bean bag, stew steaming

on the stove, kids designing outfits
for fairies on the kitchen counter,

husband clicking away online, a few
dozen snowflakes casually flying,

and the call comes. At that moment
I stand at the top of the stairs, gazing

outside at the thin limbs of aspens,
breathing and watching those fragile

crystals float down through light
from somewhere I cannot fathom.

The Gadabout

I remove my glasses and place them
on the tall dresser, safe from the kids

and foster dogs. Leave my ears beside
the bathroom sink, near the Q-tips.

Forget my mouth in the mirror, where
it remains backward. Set my neck casually

on the sill with the incense and obsidian.
Stow my breasts thoughtlessly in a drawer.

My belly, so soft and easily upset, I don't
know where to stash. I roam upstairs,

consider leaving it in a toy bin but
the entwined Barbies demand privacy

and anyhow I find myself strangely
attached. Such a stupid thing to cry about.

The Civil Engineer

Icicles drip like an IV, spilling slowly
toward the ground, growing longer

as they lose themselves. There is no
volume. I am inside, keeping even

the window at a safe distance.
I stay under the thick gray blanket

we received late, as though my mother
sent it from the grave. Despite myself

I see that ice has formed a negative
bridge across the driveway, a narrow

shining path along which no one
walks. Today, I couldn't tell a river

from a steel beam. I call to hear my
mom's voice say *I'm not here right now.*

The Prize

I can no longer hear the word
esophagus in public. I dissolve

like a slug in a pinch of salt.
But I must not dissolve. As I go,

so goes the poem, kids, perfect
family—endangered by my lack

of scrutiny, beautiful for no one.
The clinical definition of alone.

So I do school pickups, write articles,
dance, have sex—and this amnion

of easy days doesn't kill me. Perhaps
I'm carried by someone kind, therapist

or husband or by God even, the way
a girl might tote her fish in its baggie.

The Meteorologist

From the yard I watch snow
hurry to the ground, writhing, live,

thick as applesauce but white as sand
on the missile range. How far away

is heaven? How far is far enough
from earth? Here is a cold I can

cleave and cleave to. Clotted ice
compelled down, surging from cloud

to planet, from sky to my knitted hat.
What does it lose as it lands softly

on my unmittened skin? Crystalline
subjugation or liberated flight? Its fine

singularity or its loneliness? What
do I lose, returning inside?

The Dreamer

Looking up, I find no swans or spears
or ladles. Why should heaven belong

to myths, to the dead from a world
pre-tonsillectomies, pre-telescopes?

I can't remember a time before my
own mother. Why should anyone else?

Without much effort I spot myself
in the stars, a vague pattern of dots

like everything else—dipper, god, each
image created by what others imagine.

I find a child on a boat with nothing
beyond it. I find adults swarming the deck

and angry with me. But why should
I be the child and not the missing sea?

The Doctor

Hoof-prints in challenging places,
not visible on skin but obvious

on stomach, spleen, major arteries.
Buffalo, hereditary, or just horse?

Inconclusive. Brain hyperactive but
only at night. Oftentimes frozen as if

caught in a photo, or caught in "skull"
instead of skull, in "head" instead of

"body." Quote marks could be scars
from raspberry picking. Referral to

derm? Reports problems with Updike.
Amends, "Well, mostly with pretty birds."

Prescribed fish oil, long rappels, and
sharing papasan chairs with good dogs.

The Astronomer

In any darkness—a stranger's eyes,
for instance—I want to find

a night sky. Also a moon. Also
a habitable planet. I want to find

Grandma, who nursed the mentally ill,
who taught me the reason to walk

every day: to enjoy beautiful legs
when you're old. I want to find a mirror,

a mother, a destination, place of rest.
I'm shameless in my desires for other

people's grace. Today, I listen to the rain,
I read her obituary again, I wonder

what the dog is thinking. Summer is
almost here, and I'm not ready.

The Zookeeper

Love menstruating gorillas, love the straight
woman who reads lesbian fiction, love anyone

who sends love letters. The divorcee kissing
someone new for the first time in 30 years.

Those walking alone in the deep canyon,
bear spray in their packs. Love the new mom.

Love the Great Dane whose puppies are gone.
Love postmenopausal narwhals, the 4th-grader

in the catalpa tree with her crush, the broodmare
recovering from miscarriage. Love grandmother

elephants. Love married kissing, how it can
feel new, like re-reading a cherished book.

Love the ones who lie awake beside sleeping
partners, keeping vigil on an ordinary night.

The Robin

Quite early I sit up in my blue sheets
and think, *I'm no longer a child*. It's like

hitting my dry head on a waterfall.
I've loved hastily for years, and then

the universe in the shape of a dark room,
a sleeping man, and a sleep mask loose

over my nose tells me I'm fine. That
while everyone else dreams forgettable

dreams, there is just enough light for me
to see that I have a place to rest, another

to play, dogs on the rug, my daughters
upstairs, warm arms reaching toward

me. What has changed? Nothing.
Yesterday must have been the same.

Kelly Dolejsi has published poetry and fiction in numerous literary journals, including *North American Poetry Review, Denver Quarterly, The Cincinnati Review, Fifth Wednesday, The Hunger, Broken Ribbon, West Texas Literary Review, Junto, Gravel, Dirty Paws, The Hungry Chimera, Joey and the Black Boots,* and *The Disconnect.* Her poem "Loyalty" was nominated for the Best of the Net, and her contribution to the book, *September 11, 2001: American Writers Respond* (edited by William Heyen) was nominated for the Pushcart Prize. Her chapbook, *That Second Starling,* was published in 2018 by Desert Willow Press. She has also written theatrical plays, newspaper columns, and feature news stories for her local community in Los Alamos, NM. She received her MFA in Creative Writing from Emerson College in Boston.

www.ingramcontent.com/pod-product-compliance
Lightning Source LLC
Chambersburg PA
CBHW020831190426
43197CB00037B/1535